YOU CAN DO IT

GUIDE TO BETTER GRADES

by Kristine Tomasik

illustrated by Estella Hickman

*Special thanks to the teachers of
Percy Julian Junior High School, Oak Park, Illinois,
and their principal, Dr. Benjamin Williams;
also to teacher Earl Bitoy of
Emerson School, Oak Park, Illinois.*

Published by Worthington Press
7099 Huntley Road, Worthington, Ohio 43085

Printed in the United States of America

10 9 8 7 6 5 4 3

ISBN 0-87406-298-5

Contents

1
You Can Do BETTER

Why get good grades?

Face it. There are few things in life worse than sitting and stewing over the last five problems while the rest of the class is turning in their papers. Flubbing a test is not fun. And neither is turning beet red when the teacher calls on you and you don't know the answer.

And then there's the misery of taking home a bad report card. Think about those glowering looks, those phone calls to friends cut off, those curfews closing in.

Yes, there are *lots* of reasons to get good grades! Wouldn't you much rather replace bad feelings with good feelings?

Think how nice it feels to be one of the first ones to turn in your test or stick up your hand. Think of the good feeling you'll have when the paper comes back with a B or even an A on it. Think of the admiration on your classmates' faces. And think of the smiles on your parents' faces.

What's more, think of how ready you'll be for your next school! You've heard all the horror stories.

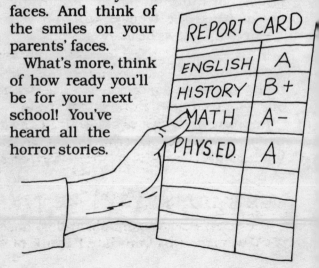

REPORT CARD	
ENGLISH	A
HISTORY	B +
MATH	A -
PHYS. ED.	A

"Ooooooo—it's soooo much tougher the next grade up! They give you eight hours of homework every night! And you have to write ten 2,000-word themes a week!"

But don't let the horror stories get to you. The next grade may be a little tougher. But it won't be that bad, especially not if you start to get your study skills ready now.

"But it's not my fault I don't get good grades!" some kids argue. That makes it sound like there's nothing you can do to improve your grades. But there really are many things you can do to get better grades.

Actually, you've already started.

You've bought this book.

With it, you'll learn a simple study key that's easy as 1–2–3. You'll use this same study key to learn how to do better in class, on your homework, and on tests.

No, you don't have to sell your life away or become a bookworm to get better grades. All it takes is a little effort every day.

THE STUDY KEY

The study key is so simple and so basic you'll wonder why you didn't think of it first. (Maybe you did!) Read it carefully, because you're going to learn to use this same key for all your studying, whether it's reading about the solar system or learning fractions.

To understand the study key, take any ordinary key out of your pocket and look at it. You'll see there are three ways to view the key.

☐ **Think big.** See the whole key.

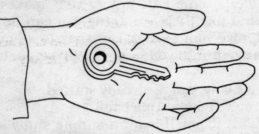

☐ **Think medium.** Break the key down into smaller parts. For example, the part you hold onto and the part you stick in the lock.

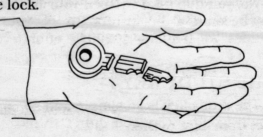

☐ **Think little.** Notice all of the little notches on the key. Those are the little details that make the key turn in the lock.

How does the study key unlock studying? Just like this. Now whenever you approach a study situation, use the key:

THINK ➡ BIG

See the big picture. Get an overview of the whole project. Ask yourself, "What's the goal?"

Let's say your big picture—your overall goal—is to read fifteen pages of your social studies textbook tonight.

THINK ➡ MEDIUM

Break it down. "Here's what I have to do to get from here to there."

9

Keeping in mind your big picture, let's say you decide to break the fifteen pages down into three segments of five pages each.

 THINK LITTLE

Next, picture how these details fit into the big picture. Everything you do is just a part of the whole. Imagine yourself moving along the key as you click off detail after detail. Do each detail as well as you can, but don't get stuck in it. If you find yourself getting frustrated over one of the details, skip it for now and go on. You can always come back to it.

For instance, as you read each sentence of each page of the five pages of the three segments of your social studies textbook, keep reminding yourself how each of these details is part of the big picture. If, for example, you find yourself getting bogged down on a certain page, remind yourself that it's just part of the whole. Skip it for now and come back to it.

THE TOOLS OF THE KEY: OUT-LINES, TO-DO LISTS, BUBBLE PICTURES, AND GRAPHS

There are a number of tools you can use to help think big, medium, and little. The tools are outlines, to-do lists, bubble pictures, and graphs.

☐ **Outlines.**

You're probably familiar with outlines. They're one way of thinking big, medium, and little. To outline that social studies textbook reading plan, for example, you'd do this:

I. FIFTEEN PAGES
   A. PAGES 1-5
   B. PAGES 6-10
   C. PAGES 11-15

(You probably wouldn't put in more details because that would take longer than reading them!)

☐ To-do list.

Maybe you've seen your mother or father make a *to-do* list, a list of things to do. You might use an arrow to mark the big tasks and indented dots to mark the medium tasks. Again, you probably wouldn't list all the details.

```
⟶ READ FIFTEEN PAGES
OF SOCIAL STUDIES
  • PAGES 1-5
  • PAGES 6-10
  • PAGES 11-15
```

☐ Bubble pictures.

Some people like to think in pictures. It's easier for them to keep in mind their big, medium, and little thinking if they can draw a picture of it.

Bubble pictures are one way to do this.

In the big bubble, write the big picture. "Read fifteen pages of social studies." Then draw a line off the bubble for every medium task.

If there are any little tasks you want to show on your bubble picture, you can write those on lines coming off of the lines. So, for example, if there's a map you need to study in pages 11–15, you'd draw a little line off of the bigger line, and write "study map."

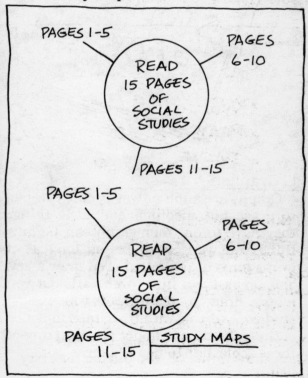

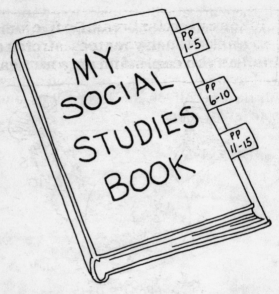

☐ Graphs.

Graphs are another way people can picture the big, medium, and little things they have to do. Your graph can be anything you want it to be—as long as it works for you! You might even draw a key, and break it up into three parts. Or you might draw a picture of your social studies textbook, with three tabs in it.

The point is not to get stuck in any of these tools, but to use whatever works to help you.

Take an exercise break. Do five jumping jacks, touch your toes, stretch as tall as you can, stand on your head.

EXERCISE BREAK

THE STUDY PATTERN

Some people set huge, impossible study goals for themselves. They start out by saying they are going to study morning, noon, and night. After a week (or a day!) they get tired and fizzle out.

Instead of overdoing it, we suggest you study in the following ways.

☐ **Same time, same place.** Set a regular time and place for your studying. Include both a time to begin *and* a time to end. You might decide to study every day from four to six P.M. at your study desk in your room.

SAME TIME
SAME PLACE

12:00

☐ **Bite-sized chunks.** Don't try to do it all at once. You eat every day, three times a day, don't you? You need to think the same way about studying. Your studying has to be regular and meal-sized.

It's better to have a two- or three-hour study time five days a week than one ten-hour cram session.

☐ **Make a plan.**
Think big, think medium, think little. Which homework do you have to get done tonight? How much time do you have to study overall? How much time will you give to each of the smaller tasks? What order will you do them in?

For example, you may decide to devote the first hour to math, while you're still fresh, the next half-hour to language arts, and finish up with a half-hour of history.

□ **Pace yourself.** As you work, check the clock every once in a while to see how you are doing. Don't be rigid about your time schedule, but be aware of it.

□ **Change your pace if necessary.** You might decide halfway through your study time that you need to change your pace or your plan. For instance, you might realize that you really didn't allow enough time for the social studies reading. That's okay. You may want to change your pace by speeding up to finish the social studies. Or you may decide to change your plan and allow more time for social studies and less time for something else.

☐ **Keep your studying varied.** Do some math, then do some language arts, then do some history. Don't try to do all history one night or all language arts the next. That could be too boring.

☐ **Keep your studying fun.** Take regular but short breaks while you study. Every 45 minutes to an hour, take a 5- to 10-minute break and do something fun. We've suggested some ideas for study breaks throughout this book to get you into the habit.

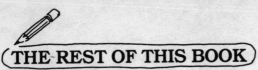

THE REST OF THIS BOOK

The rest of this book is divided according to the three basic study situations you'll find yourself in now and in the future:

1. In class
2. At home
3. Taking tests

As we go along, we'll explain how the study key fits each of these basic study situations.

Stop now and take a look at the table of contents to see what specific study skills fall under each heading. For instance, you'll see that reading textbooks and writing papers are both study skills explained under the "at home" heading. (You'll notice that when you skim through the table of contents, you are using the study key. You are "thinking big" by getting an overview of the book.)

And we've included a special box at the end of each section to help you make the switch to the next grade.

So read on. You can do it! You can get better grades.

Take a dance break. Turn on your favorite music and dance. You'll feel great when you go back to your desk.

DANCE BREAK

21

2
You Can Do Better IN CLASS

BE THERE

Getting better grades almost always begins in class. Be there! That may sound simple, but it's probably the most important thing you can do to help yourself get good grades.

"Oh, I can do it on my own" or "They're not discussing anything important today, anyway," or "It won't hurt to miss just this once" are dangerous ways of thinking. You never know what you might miss if you are not in class. You might miss some important instructions for doing a paper, or even a casual comment by another classmate about the reading. You never know! Something might happen!

If you're lying in bed, wondering if you should fake being sick and not go to school, *go*. It's better to go than not to go.

BE THERE ON TIME

Are you one of those people who comes flying in the classroom door at the last second? You don't mean to be late, but "time just gets away" from you?

This won't make your teacher too happy. At the worst, you might even get tardy marks, which could affect the grade you get.

How do you get to class on time?

Start by getting to school on time! Have you ever noticed how a day you begin by running late never quite catches up? That's why it's so important to start on time. And that means *getting up on time*!

Be realistic about what time you need to get up. Use the chart below to help you figure it out. Start with the time you must be in the first class at school, and figure backward. When is that first bell? What do you have to do before you go to class? Go to your locker? Talk to friends?

How long does it really take you to get to school? Write down what time you must leave the house.

What things do you have to do before you leave the house, and how long does it take you to do them? Be honest, now! You probably have to get dressed, eat breakfast, and maybe make your lunch. Figure out how much time these things really take you and write down what time you have to get up. Be sure to allow a couple minutes for yawning and stretching! A tip: you may be able to help yourself out in the morning if you pack your book bag and choose your clothes the night before.

Get up at: __7:15__

* take shower -takes __15__ min.
* get dressed - takes __10__ min.
* eat breakfast -takes __10__ min.
* make lunch- takes __10__ min.
* other   -takes __5__ min.

Leave house at: __8:05__

* walk, ride bike, ride bus-
   takes __10__ min.

Arrive at School at: __8:15__

* go to locker -takes __2__ min.
* talk to friends-takes __5__ min.

First Bell for first class is at: __8:27__

This might seem like a lot of scheduling, but it's worth it! Soon you'll get into the habit of being on time.

Then, all you have to do is keep it up the rest of the day. Just look at the clock between classes. Note when it's time for you to go, and just go. Don't hang around talking. A simple "See you later" is a polite enough way to leave.

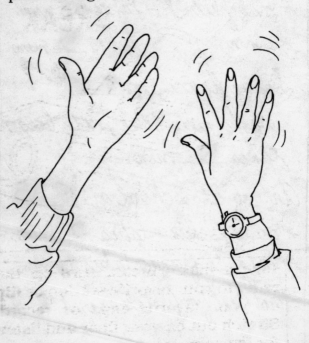

MUSIC BREAK

Take a music break. Turn on the radio to your favorite station or flip on your favorite tape or record. Stretch out on your floor and listen for five minutes.

BE THERE PREPARED

Has this ever happened to you? Just as you sit down in class you realize, "Oh, no! I haven't got a pen!" or "I brought the wrong notebook!"

If your books, papers, and notebooks are scattered everywhere, you'll never be quite mentally present in class, even if your body's there.

So get organized. You need:

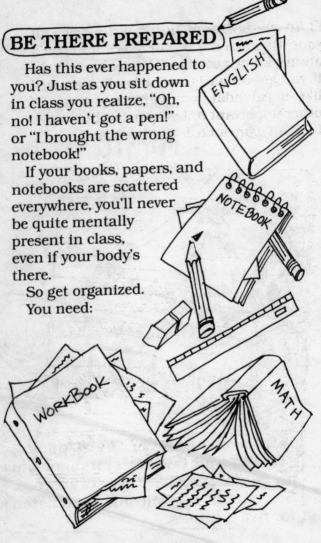

☐ **An assignment book.** Write down all your assignments in one place and you'll always know exactly what you have to do. If you get an assignment book organized like a calendar, you can keep track of other important dates—parties, birthdays, football games, etc.!

```
        MONDAY  OCT. 17, 1988
7:00  Get up!
8:00  School Starts
9:00
10:00
11:00
12:00 Lunch
1:00
2:00
3:00  Meet Judy and Diane
4:00      at the Mall
5:00
6:00  Pizza with Mom and Dad
7:00
8:00
9:00  Home - Call Judy about
10:00     the party on Friday
11:00
12:00
Comments: Stop and get notebook
paper for English.
```

☐ **A three-ring notebook.** Buy or make dividers for each of your subjects. And buy lots of notebook paper for your notes! Your three-ring notebook will be the backbone of your class work. Keep all your class notes, and any notes you take on homework assignments in this notebook.

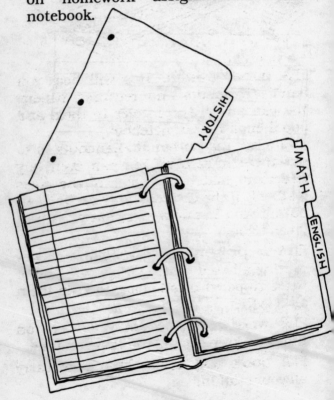

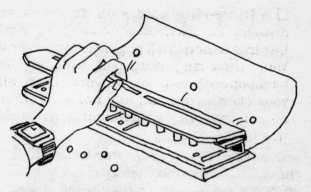

☐ **A paper punch.** This will help you handle handouts and returned papers. You can punch three holes in them and pop them into your notebook.

Another way to handle handouts is to put them in folders. You can even buy folders to match the color of the class textbook. If the textbook is green, you can put all your handouts for that class in a green folder.

☐ **Pens or pencils.** You might consider putting all your writing tools into one of those zippered plastic bags to keep them all together.

☐ **A wristwatch**—to get you there on time and keep getting you there on time.

☐ **A book bag or backpack**—to carry all your stuff in.

BE THERE MENTALLY

Applying the Study Key to Class

We've been talking about being in class physically. That's number one.

But you have to be there mentally, too.

Use the study key to help you. As you enter each class, sit down and get yourself ready. *Think big, think medium, think little!* "I am in history class. We are studying the American Revolution. Today the teacher is going to be talking about the Battle of Bunker Hill."

If your teacher has given you a course outline, take a look at that, too. It will help you see where you are.

It sounds simple, but that's the beauty of the study key. You'll be amazed at how much it helps you be ready for whatever the class holds.

HOW TO LISTEN

Besides being there, listening is the second most important thing you can do in class. Here are a few listening tips.

☐ Sit in the front.
If you have a choice, try to get a seat near or in the front. This way you can keep eye contact with the teacher and stay really involved.

If you have to sit in the back, watch the teacher closely. Keeping your eyes on the teacher will help you keep your ears on him or her, too.

☐ **Concentrate.** Really hear what the teacher is saying. Set your mind on listening. Put some energy into it!

☐ **Focus on the main point.** Use the study key. As you listen to each sentence the teacher says, you'll be "thinking little." But in your mind, step back every couple minutes or so to "think big." Ask yourself: "What's the main point so far? What is she driving at?"

For instance, suppose your teacher has been giving you example after example of industries dumping pollution into rivers and streams. You could get so lost in the examples that you forget the main point. The teacher may be trying to get you to see that laws controlling pollution need to be enforced.

☐ **Deal directly with distractions.** Everyone's mind wanders now and then. In the middle of class, you may suddenly think "Oh, Mom said I had to feed the cats when I got home." Make a note of the distracting thought in your assignment book or "to-do" list. Then forget it for now.

Handle your personal problems before or after class. There's nothing that can make you lose your concentration faster than just having had a fight with your best friend or your parents. Try to solve your personal problems as soon as possible—before or after class. If you let them drag on, they will drag you down. Sometimes personal problems—even little ones—get so big they seem to take over. If you are feeling overwhelmed by personal or emotional issues, get some help. You may want to talk to your parents or your friends. Or you might think about seeing the school counselor about your problem.

☐ **Don't forget your body.** Listening closely is hard for your body. When you listen closely, your body tends to stay in one position. Your blood circulation slows down and you start to feel sleepy. So give your body a break every so often. Shift in your seat, without distracting anyone. Do an exercise, like pushing your hands together hard, or tightening and then relaxing different parts of your body. This will keep the blood flowing and prevent you from feeling tired.

Take a joke break. Think of the two funniest jokes you know. Or read two comic strips from today's paper. Give yourself a laugh!

HOW TO TAKE NOTES

Taking good notes in class is a great way to remember what the teacher thinks is important. Good notes will help you learn the subject, prepare for the next day's class, and do well on tests.

To take good notes, be sure you have the supplies mentioned earlier. Is your three-ring binder open? Do you have plenty of paper ready? Are your pencils sharpened?

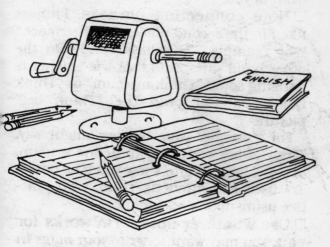

☐ **Note openers.** Most teachers will start their lectures by telling you what they are going to tell you. Any good speaker knows this rule of thumb: "Tell them what you're going to tell them. Then tell them. Then tell them what you told them." It's just like the study key. Your teacher starts out by giving you the big picture. For instance, she may say, "Today I'm going to talk about nouns." Write down "nouns" and keep it in mind as you listen. Pretend you are making a drawing or a map. You are translating the map in the teacher's mind onto the paper in front of you.

☐ **Note connecting phrases.** Phrases like: "In the second place," "Furthermore," "For example," "Similarly," and "On the other hand" are hints that the teacher is hanging some "Think medium" or "Think little" material onto the "Think big" picture.

For example, your teacher might say, "First of all, I'm going to define a noun. Second, I'm going to show you how nouns are used in sentences. Third, we'll practice using nouns in sentences."

☐ **Use whatever note form works for you.** You may want to write your notes in an outline form, or you might want to use one of the tools mentioned earlier: bubble pictures or "to-do" lists.

Here is a small part of one teacher's lecture on the constellations (star formations) of winter. Following it are one student's notes on this part of the lecture.

Winter Constellations

The sky is clearest on cold, bright winter nights. You can see the winter constellations very clearly then. And you can even pick out some of the fainter stars not usually seen when the air is less clear.

The winter constellations center on Orion, the Hunter. According to Greek myths, Orion boasted that no animals could overcome him.

You can use Orion to find other winter constellations. The belt of Orion acts as a pointer. To the northwest, it points toward Taurus, the Bull.

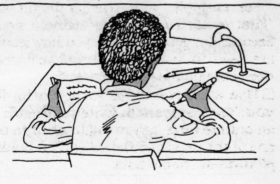

Here are the student's notes on this part of the lecture.

Winter — best time to see
          stars
• sky clear
• can see fainter stars

Orion — central winter
          constellation
• called "the Hunter"
• boasted that no
animal could overcome him

Use Orion to find other
          constellations
• belt used as a
          pointer
• points to the north-
west to Taurus, the Bull

☐ **Note what your teacher thinks is important.** Again, most teachers will give you hints about what they really think is important. They may be very blunt. They may say something like: "Now, this will be on the test!" or, "Make sure you get this!"

Some teachers will be a little less obvious. They may say something twice—in exactly the same words, or using different words. Again, you should take note of that information.

And don't forget to watch body language—what your teacher says without words. If your teacher is waving his arms around as he makes a point, he probably is saying something he really wants you to remember.

☐ **Use visual aids.** Draw stars, underlines, or arrows to call attention to things that are important. You may want to use all capital letters, question marks, or squiggly lines. Or you may want to use highlighting markers. Use whatever works for you.

☐ **Catch key words.** Don't try to write down every word the teacher says. You're not a human tape recorder! It's most important that you catch and write down key phrases—verbs and nouns. Don't bother with words like of, with, at, and, but, the. Or if you do, use shorthand symbols:

@	for	*at*
+ n &	for	*and*
w/	for	*with*
w/o	for	*without*
i.e.	for	*for example*

☐ **Borrow notes if you miss class.** If you *have* to be absent, ask to borrow notes from a friend who takes good ones. You'll not only get the information, you might get a few hints about notetaking from the way your friend takes notes. And be sure to return the favor when your friend needs to use your notes.

RELATIONSHIP RULES

Relationships are one of the most important things in the world. You won't get very far if you don't have a good working relationship with your teachers.

☐ **Be friendly.** A smile on your face is far more inviting to a teacher than a frown. It may not influence your grade, but it will certainly make your time in class more enjoyable.

☐ **Be polite.** At the least, be polite. Say "Mr." or "Ms." when you talk to the teacher. Don't butt in when the teacher is speaking. Don't whisper or goof off in class. Don't argue with the teacher in front of the other kids (unless, of course, you're supposed to as part of a class debate or discussion).

□ **Don't expect a comedian.** Teachers were hired because they are good teachers, not because they are stand-up comics. You might find one who is as good at cracking a joke as teaching. But don't count on it. Teachers have many interesting and valuable things to tell you, even if they don't have a joke every other line.

□ **Don't be put off.** Every once in a while, you'll find a teacher who seems gruff or growly. Don't let it scare you. Teachers are usually teachers because they care about teaching you. Keep being friendly to this teacher and he or she may warm up some.

□ **Don't butter up the teacher.** Being friendly is different than being gushy. Being friendly means being sincere. Be nice not just to try to butter up the teacher.

□ **What if you really feel that your teacher doesn't like you?** Well, that does happen. But it's still no reason not to follow the above relationship rules— especially the "be polite" one. You just never know. You might win the teacher over yet.

RELAXATION BREAK

Take a relaxation break. Turn off all noise and lights. Lie down on the floor. Take deep breaths and go into that still, quiet part of yourself. Relax. (Be careful not to fall asleep.)

Teacher Style

Not every teacher runs his or her class the same way. Different teachers expect different things. Right now, you may have only one teacher, or maybe two or three. Soon you may have as many as six or seven. Learning early what the teacher expects will help you meet their different expectations.

Most teachers come in three styles: talkers, discussers, and doers.

☐ **Talkers.** These are the teachers who like to do the talking. They often want you to spit back on the test exactly what they've said in class.

☐ **Discussers.** These teachers like a lot of class discussion. You are supposed to learn in their classes by sharing ideas and talking about them. These teachers are hoping to teach you to think for yourself. On their tests, they like you to reason on your own instead of just recalling the facts they've given.

☐ **Doers.** These teachers tend to teach classes that are project- or skill-oriented. Typing, art, physical education, shop, and science teachers tend to be like this. Their emphasis is not so much on what you say as what you do. Can you make that jump shot? How many words per minute can you crank out on the typewriter? How did your lab experiment turn out? Your performance is what counts most.

Of course, some teachers will be combinations of these three basic types.

HOW TO TALK

Speaking up in class, taking part in class discussions, and asking questions are very important skills for every class, no matter what the teacher's style. Some teachers will want you to talk more in class than other teachers will. But you still need these talking skills for each class. Here's how to open your mouth without getting your foot stuck in it.

☐ **Listen.** To take part in a discussion, you have to know what's going on. That means listening. Try to follow the flow of the conversation. Then, when you're ready, make your comment.

☐ **Speak Up.** Speak clearly and boldly. If you mumble, no one will be able to hear you. When you have something to say, say it. Don't let others keep cutting you off.

☐ **Keep it short.** Make your comments clear and to the point. Explain yourself fully, but don't talk on and on.

☐ **Don't be a floor hog.** Don't try to show off or take over the discussion. Be polite enough not to interrupt other people, steal their ideas, or finish their sentences.

☐ **Build on what others have said.** If you are having a hard time coming up with something to say in the discussion, try building on what others have said. Do you agree with their ideas? Do you disagree? Does something they've said give you an idea? Open your mouth and speak up.

☐ **Ask.** Sometimes your teacher says something that doesn't make sense to you. Maybe it's directions for a homework assignment or maybe it's a point in the teacher's lecture. You may feel dumb, but if you're not getting the teacher's meaning, *ask*. Ask the teacher to explain further. But be polite about it. Say something like: "I'm sorry, I don't understand. Could you explain a little more about—?"

You probably won't be the only one who was wondering! Other kids probably did, too, but they were too shy to ask.

What if you really feel too silly asking your question in class? What if the teacher has rushed on to other material and you feel it wouldn't be appropriate to interrupt? Then go up after class and ask. You deserve to have your question answered, especially if it's about directions from homework or a test.

HOW TO REMEMBER

We'll be working more on memory and memorizing in the "Taking Tests" part of this book. But you'll help yourself a lot if you practice a few simple memory tasks now before you get to test time.

☐ **Think big.** A few minutes before each class ends, stop thinking little and go back to thinking big. Ask yourself, "What was this class about?" See if you can give a one-sentence or one-phrase summary. For example: "This class was about the skeletal structure of the human body."

☐ **Review.** If you did take notes in the class, review them very quickly as soon after class as you can. Just glance over them once in study hall, homeroom, on the bus going home, or as you start your homework for the evening.

☐ **Summarize.** Try this handy recall trick. Get a 3″ x 5″ card for each class, kind of like a flash card. See if you can summarize the day's class with one trigger word. So if you spent the day in language arts talking about the character of Margaret in Judy Blume's *Are You There God? It's Me, Margaret.*, you'd write "Margaret" on your card. Keep this up and you'll have a summary at a glance of what went on in class.

MOVING AHEAD

Probably the hardest switch you'll make when you move ahead to the next grade is that you'll have more teachers to pay attention to and learn to understand. In grade school you may have had only one or two teachers, and you got used to them gradually, over the first semester.

In your next school, you may only have your teachers for a semester. And you're likely to encounter six or seven personalities a day. You have to get used to more variety—quicker.

It might help you to actually make a chart of your teachers. Make one sheet of paper at the front of your three-ring notebook to jot down "teacher characteristics." You don't have to analyze your teachers, but just jot down observations about the way they are and what they seem to like and dislike. You might write: "Stern. Really hates people who whisper." Or, "Neat. Wants assignments with one-inch margins all the way around." Or, "Talkative. Grades on number of comments made in class."

Well, after watching the minute hand creep around the last five minutes, the bell has finally rung, and you're out the door! Congratulations! You've had a very successful day at school. You were there! You listened. You took good notes. And you've quickly reviewed them in your spare moments. You're on your way to getting better grades.

NATURE BREAK

Take a nature break. Get back in touch with nature. Go outside and sniff the air. Pick up some earth and rub it between your fingers. Feel a leaf. Look at the stars.

3
You Can Do Better AT HOME

It's 3:30 or 4:00, and you're home from school. You walk in the door, toss your jacket one direction, and your book bag another, and grab a glass of milk.

You'd really like to go outside and shoot a couple of baskets. But you know you have at least two hours of homework to do before tomorrow. Well, maybe you can do it tonight—ooo—but there's that special program you want to watch on TV tonight!

Decisions, decisions.

Most of life is about making decisions. When you choose to do one thing, you are often choosing not to do another. You try to strike a balance. Making decisions about the time to do your homework is no different. By learning how to plan to do your homework, you'll be practicing a skill you'll use all your life. Planning when to do your homework will help you make sure it gets done—and this will help you get good grades.

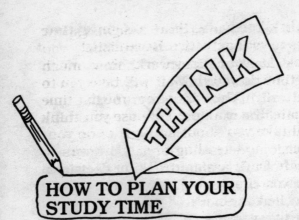

HOW TO PLAN YOUR STUDY TIME

Applying the Study Key to Homework

By now you're probably familiar with the study key—*Think big, think medium, think little.* How does it apply to planning your homework?

☐ **Think big.** How many total hours do you have between now and the time you want to go to bed? Let's say it's 4:00 when you get home from school. You want to go to bed at 10:00. That's a total of six hours.

Write "six hours" at the top of your planning page. Jot down all the things you want to and need to do between now and when you want to go to bed. Include your homework, fun stuff, making phone calls, eating dinner, doing any chores you might have, and getting ready for bed.

☐ **Think medium.** Start assigning time values to your activities. Be realistic!

Look at your homework. How much total time do you think it will take you to do it all? This is your rough time estimate. For example, suppose you think it will take you about an hour to do your language arts reading and two hours to do your math assignment. That's a total of three hours.

Now look at some of the other things you want to do. How long could each of them take? For instance, you know you usually spend about an hour when you go out to shoot baskets. Supper with your family lasts about an hour, too, when you figure in your chores. And it really takes you about an hour to un-wind and get ready for bed. The TV show you want to watch is also an hour long.

☐ **Think little.** Start adding up the time totals of what you want to do. Does it add up to the total time you have? If not, does something need to get bumped?

Look at your larger tasks, like homework, more closely. Break them down into smaller parts and assign times to those parts. Was your original rough estimate accurate? If not, how do you need to readjust your schedule?

For example, if you add up the sample time totals above, you can see you'd be in trouble. You've got seven hours of things to do and only six hours to do them. Either you'd have to go to bed an hour later, or else cut out one hour's worth of activities. (*Hint:* don't kid yourself into thinking you can squeeze three hours of homework into two.)

MONDAY SUBJECT	TIME TO DO STUDIES	TOTAL TIME 6 HOURS
MATH	2 HOURS	4 HOURS
ENGLISH	3 HOURS	1 HOUR
HISTORY	2 HOURS	-1 HOUR
SOCCER	1 HOUR	-2 HOURS

58

Play with the parts and the pieces until you come up with a workable schedule. Workable means a schedule *you* can live with! Workable does *not* mean you schedule every second! Workable does *not* mean you don't allow yourself any fun!

Workable does mean that you might have to choose. Either you go outside *or* you watch the TV show. Workable means that you set some limits on your homework. Sometimes, setting limits helps you be more efficient during the time you're working on your homework. If you say, "I will work on my homework from 6:00 to 8:00," you tend to stay more alert during that time. If you think, "This is just going to drag on forever!"—it probably will.

You may copy the study planning sheet on page 63 to help you plan your study time.

Here are some more tips for setting up a workable study schedule.

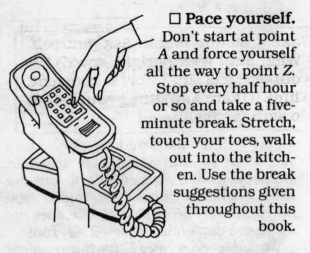

☐ **Pace yourself.** Don't start at point A and force yourself all the way to point Z. Stop every half hour or so and take a five-minute break. Stretch, touch your toes, walk out into the kitchen. Use the break suggestions given throughout this book.

☐ **Keep it varied.** Unless you absolutely have to, don't work on one subject for so long that you get bored with it. Do quickly but well what you have to do—then move on to the next subject.

☐ **Give yourself rewards.** Tell yourself, "When I get to the end of five pages, I can have one chocolate chip cookie." Or, "When I've worked out the first ten problems, I can make one five-minute phone call to Laurie." You can use the ideas in the study breaks that are scattered throughout this book as rewards, too.

Take a feeling break. Ask yourself, "What am I feeling right now?" Let yourself feel that for a moment. Think if there's anything you need to do with the feeling.

Consider studying at exactly the same time each day. Make studying a good habit. It you know that at exactly 6:30 each evening you are going to sit down and study, it becomes kind of like a buzzer in your head. Six-thirty comes, the buzzer goes off in your head, and your body knows what to do: go sit down and start studying. If you have trouble disciplining yourself to study, this may be the best route for you.

Study planning sheet

Total time I have: _____hours
  (from _____P.M. to _____P.M.)

Fun things I want to do in this time:	How long each thing will take to do:
Studying I need to do during this time:	How long each study task will take:

I need to bump:

I need to refigure:

Finished schedule that is workable for me:

  Clock time: Activity:

HOW TO PLAN YOUR STUDY PLACE

Having a place to study is just as important as planning time to study.

What's the best kind of study place?

Most students find that they need five basic things in their study space: a desk, a chair, a lamp, supplies, and QUIET.

☐ **Desk.** The best desk is a clean one. No matter whether your desk is an office-type desk or a simple small table, you'll get nowhere if it's cluttered. So keep it cleaned off.

What kind of a desk should you have?

You can buy a simple, inexpensive student desk, or you can make your own desk. Try placing a smooth board across two low filing cabinets or crates. Or look for an old table in the basement or at a garage sale (or find an old desk!).

☐ **Chair.** You can use a folding chair, an old kitchen or dining room chair, or you can purchase an inexpensive desk chair. If you want to get fancier, you might be able to find at a garage sale an old secretary's chair—the kind with wheels and an adjustable back.

☐ **Light.** A simple
single desk lamp
will work well. You
could also use an
inexpensive clamp-
on light from the
hardware store.

☐ **Supplies.** Be sure to have all your supplies right at hand. There's nothing worse
than getting all settled at your desk,
opening your math book, and then dis-
covering you don't have a pencil. You have
to jump up and waste five minutes rum-
maging around the kitchen looking for
one. By the time you get back to your
desk, you've lost not only time, but
energy.

So have your supplies all there:
☐ pencils
☐ pens
☐ erasers
☐ paper
☐ clock
☐ dictionary

Other supplies you might want to have
include:
- scissors
- tape
- paper clips
- stapler
- ruler or other
  straight edge
- calculator

Keep your supplies in your desk
drawer. If your desk doesn't have a drawer
in it, you might want to get a silverware
holder like the kind your mom has in her
kitchen drawer. They make a great box for
keeping your pens, pencils, etc. separated.
You can keep your paper in an empty typing paper box.

□ **Quiet.** Some people say that they study
best with background noise. That may be.
But sitting in the middle of the kitchen
with brothers and sisters screaming and
fighting all around you is probably not
going to work for anyone. Most of us need
some degree of quiet.

Where you locate your desk/study area
will probably determine how much quiet
you get. If you have your own room, you
can probably find a quiet space there. If
not, see if there's any unused, quiet cor-

ner of the house where you could set up your study spot. Have you thought of the basement? How about the attic? Maybe there's even a large, walk-in closet somewhere in your house that you could use.

If you must study in a noisy spot, try plugging yourself in to a personal mini stereo with headphones. It will block the outside noise. (Just be sure the music you choose to listen to isn't just as distracting to you as the noise!)

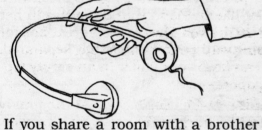

If you share a room with a brother or sister, your room can still work as a study place. You and your brother or sister just have to agree on some system of quiet time for study. Maybe you will both decide to study at the same time and be very quiet together. Maybe you will decide that one of you has study hours from 4 to 6, the other from 7 to 9. Each of you can agree to leave the room when it's not your study hours.

There are many ways you and your brother or sister can work it out. Just talk it over honestly with each other. Agree on a plan and try it for a week or so. You may even want to write up your agreement in the form of a contract. At the end of the week, see how it's going. Make any adjustments you need to in your plan. You can work it out together!

> Take a friend break. Okay, you can let yourself call a friend on the phone. When you begin the conversation, say, "Hi, I can only talk for five minutes." Then stick to it.

FRIEND BREAK

Your Learning Style

It's a pretty safe guess that most of us do our best work when there's peace and quiet. But there are those few rare individuals who actually can study best with some background noise—a TV or radio, for instance.

That's because they have a different *learning style* from the rest of us.

A *learning style* describes the conditions that you do your best studying or learning under. Besides sound, there are a number of other things that influence how well you do or don't learn. Here are a few.

☐ **Light.** Some people study best in dim light. Others need bright glare to do their best.

☐ **Temperature.** If the room is too cool some people can't concentrate. Others have that trouble if it's too warm.

☐ **Space.** Some people like a large, open space. Others prefer a small, cozy one.

☐ **Solitude.** Some students do their best studying alone. Other students find they think and learn best in the company of other people.

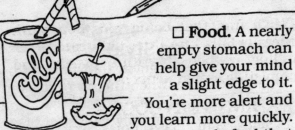

☐ **Food.** A nearly empty stomach can help give your mind a slight edge to it. You're more alert and you learn more quickly. On the other hand, some people find that a small snack now and then keeps their brain cells refueled.

☐ **Time of Day.** Are you a morning person? Some students find they can get up in the wee hours of dawn and do their best on their homework. Others find they do best in the afternoon or early evening.

All of these are factors in your learning style. So the next time your studying isn't going the greatest, stop a minute and think about your learning style. Are you a cool-room person in a hot house? Do you need to have bright light to study or dim light?

Experiment a little with different learning styles. You may discover yours is not what you thought it was!

Okay, your study schedule and study place are all set. You've got your desk, papers, and pencils ready. You're ready to do your homework!

You'll find that doing your homework generally falls into three skill categories: reading textbooks, writing papers, and completing assignments or handouts.

READING TEXTBOOKS

Besides your class notes, your textbooks or other assigned readings are your most important sources of information about the class subject. You'll be reading your textbooks to learn about many different topics.

Once more, you can use the study key to help you read more quickly and more efficiently.

Applying the Study Key to Reading

☐ **Think big.** Look over the entire reading you're assigned from beginning to end. Read the headings and the subheadings. Look at any graphs, pictures, captions, or charts. By surveying the chapter like this, you're building a kind of mental map of it.

It's also a good idea to do this kind of "big picture" thinking with the entire textbook when you first get it. Look at the table of contents. How is the book organized generally? Where does it seem to be going?

☐ **Think medium.** Look at the questions at the end of the reading before you begin. These questions often cover the main ideas the author wants you to get. Keep these in mind.

If there are no questions, sometimes there will be a chapter preview that covers the main ideas. It tells you what the reading is going to be about. Again, be sure to zero in on the main ideas that will be coming.

☐ **Think little.** Read the assignment, section by section. Keep the big picture in mind as you do. Keep reminding yourself how this particular section fits into the whole.

Reading a textbook for school is very different from reading a book for fun. When you read for fun, you can let your mind go and get lost in the details of the story. But you need to read a textbook in a different way. Keep your mind alert, and stay up on top. Read a section quickly and for understanding. Then stop and ask yourself if you know what you've read. If you find yourself getting sleepy, take a break. Get up and stretch and move around a little.

Remembering What You Read

Using the study key will get you off on the right foot in your textbook readings. You'll get the big picture before you start, and you'll stay alert as you move through the details.

But remembering what you read is just as important as reading it. It won't help at all to do your reading the night before if you can't remember a single thing you read when you get to class. Here are a few tips on remembering.

☐ **Underline or highlight.** If you own your books, underline the key points. You might want to use a two-color system. You could use a yellow highlighter for important material, and an orange or pink one for very important material.

☐ **Take notes.** If you do not own your textbooks, take notes on your reading. The point of note-taking is not to recopy the text. Instead, you will want to note main ideas in short, key phrases. Here's a sample textbook reading and notes that were taken on it.

SAMPLE TEXTBOOK READING:

What Is Geography?

The word geography comes from two Greek words, which together mean "the charting of the Earth." But geography is much more than that. Geography is not only the study of the Earth's surface, but also of the resources found above, on, and below the surface of this planet. It is the study of how people use the Earth's resources. It is the study of how the environment affects the way people live and how people affect the environment.

There are many types of geography. Physical geography studies the planet Earth and its place in the universe. A physical geographer is concerned with the study of soils, plants and animals, minerals, and weather. He or she is also concerned about the different forms which land, sea, and air take.

Economic geography is the study of how people make a living from the Earth and its resources. An economic geographer is concerned with the resources taken from the Earth and the uses of those resources by humans. The economic geographer may study everything from boat-making in India to sheep-grazing in northern Europe to trade between countries.

Cultural geography studies the ways people live in different environments. It looks at how groups of people are related. It also looks at how groups of people are related to the locations in which they live.

Strategic geography is the study of how people can make the best use of resources to allow them to survive and to improve themselves. A strategic geographer might help select the best possible place to put a factory and the number of people needed to work there. He or she might also study the importance of that factory to the survival of the country. The strategic geographer would be concerned about the resources needed by a country which can be gotten only from other countries. She or he would also help plan for national defense by studying the geographic features of this country and other countries.

Taken from Introduction to the Social Sciences by John Jay Bonstingl. © 1980 by Allyn and Bacon. pp. 273, 274.

75

NOTES:

★ **GEOGRAPHY** – STUDY OF EARTH'S SURFACE
- EARTH'S RESOURCES
- HOW PEOPLE USE RESOURCES
- HOW ENVIRONMENT AFFECTS PEOPLE
- HOW PEOPLE AFFECT ENVIRONMENT

★ **PHYSICAL GEOGRAPHY**
- PLANTS AND ANIMALS
- MINERALS
- WEATHER

★ **ECONOMIC GEOGRAPHY**
- THE STUDY OF EARTH'S RESOURCES AND HOW PEOPLE USE THEM

★ **CULTURAL GEOGRAPHY**
- STUDY OF HOW PEOPLE LIVE IN DIFFERENT ENVIRONMENTS

★ **STRATEGIC GEOGRAPHY**
- STUDY OF HOW TO MAKE THE BEST USE OF RESOURCES

Write your notes in outline form, or use the bubble system. Try to keep your notes very short and to the point.

You will probably want to write your notes as you go along. Then go back over them quickly when you're done with the reading to make sure you understand what you meant and to make sure you haven't forgotten to include some important point.

☐ **Draw a diagram.** Another way of understanding your reading is to draw a diagram of it. Read the whole reading. Then draw a diagram or map of it (sometimes called a "flow chart"). Begin with where the reading began. Then draw arrows to show where the ideas went.

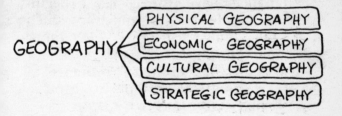

GEOGRAPHY
- PHYSICAL GEOGRAPHY
- ECONOMIC GEOGRAPHY
- CULTURAL GEOGRAPHY
- STRATEGIC GEOGRAPHY

☐ **Review.** When you finish your reading, go over the main ideas in either your notes or in your textbook.

☐ **Speak.** Close the textbook or shut your notebook. Try to put the main ideas into your own words, out loud. If you feel dumb talking to yourself, call a friend. Or corner your little brother or sister and give them a mini-talk.

☐ **Summarize.** Summarize the main points of the reading in about three or four key words. Write the words on a 3" x 5" card or in a convenient place in your three-ring notebook. Then, when you get to class tomorrow, a quick glance at your summary will trigger your memory.

WRITING PAPERS

All papers have three parts: a beginning, a middle, and an end (very much like the study key—*think big, think medium, think little.*)

The *beginning*, or *"lead"* sentence, is where you state your topic or capture your reader's attention.

The *middle*, the *"body,"* is where you develop your topic. It's made up of paragraphs, and guess what? Paragraphs also have a beginning, a middle, and an end. Pretty neat, huh?

The *end* is your *"conclusion,"* where you wrap up the ideas you developed in your paper.

The worst part about any writing is getting started. So—let's get going!

Choosing a Topic

A lot of students get stuck right here. The teacher tells you to write about anything you want. Or worse, she assigns a topic. But the topic is too narrow and boring for you.

In either case, you should find something to write about that excites you.

If your teacher has left the topic wide open, then try *free association* to get your ideas rolling. Let your mind go into a sort of daydream state, and just start writing down whatever comes into it for about five minutes. Sooner or later, your mind is going to come up with some great subjects. And you'll be there to grab them and run when it does.

If your teacher has given you a topic, see if you can find some "angle" on it that interests you and that your teacher will let you write about. For example, suppose you've been assigned to write about how blood circulates in the human body—in other words, about the circulatory system. Could you imagine that you are one of the red blood cells, and describe in detail your journey?

Using the Library

It's fun to go to the library, but sometimes it can seem downright confusing. But it's not, really, if you just remember one very important person and a few simple tools.

The important person is the librarian. The librarian is there to help you figure out how to find information. If you have a question, just ask. Librarians expect people to ask questions.

☐ **The catalog.** Every book in the library is listed in a catalog. Some libraries have card catalogs with drawers full of 3″ x 5″ cards. Catalogs in other libraries are on microfiche or on a computer. Subjects, book titles, and authors are arranged in alphabetical order, from A to Z. You can find books on your topic by looking up the subject in the catalog.

For example, you could look up "circulatory system." Under circulatory system, there will be all the books the library has about the circulatory system. While you're at it, remember to look up any related words you can think of (for example, "blood" or "heart" or "veins"). Sometimes one listing will lead you to another. In the information about one book, you may read the words, "See also. . . ." Then you can look up what it says to "see also."

If the catalog is all on a computer, you may need the librarian's help to learn how to use the computer. Again, all you need to do is ask.

☐ **The *Reader's Guide to Periodical Literature.*** These books will help you find magazine articles. The books are called the *"Reader's Guide"* for short. They are indexes of magazine articles by topic. Get the *Reader's Guide* with the most recent date on it. Then look up your topic words, just like you did in the card catalog. You can ask the librarian how to find the magazines you want.

☐ **The encyclopedia.** There's a third useful tool you should always check when you come to the library to do research. That's an encyclopedia. You'll get a good overview of any topic in the encyclopedia.

Taking Notes on the Information

It's a good idea to gather your information by taking notes on what you read. Some people like to write their notes on 3″ x 5″ cards, one idea to a card. Other people like to write their notes on regular-sized sheets of paper. They find that a card is too small for what they want to remember.

If a page or part of an article or book is really good, you might want to just photocopy the page instead of trying to copy it all down.

A tip: Don't try to read every book or article the library has on the subject! Limit yourself to several of the best instead. Then gather *enough* information —not too much, or you'll feel swamped— and not too little, or your paper will not contain enough information.

Organizing the Information

You've gotten all the information you need, and noted it on cards or paper. Now—what to do with it?

Organize!

You might start by actually arranging your cards or sheets of paper. You can even spread them out on the floor if you

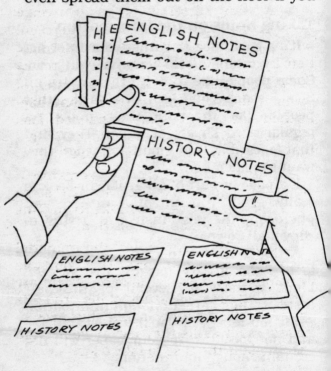

like. Organizing your ideas for a paper is just like putting together a picture puzzle. So shuffle your cards, move them around, see what might fit where. You don't have to make a final decision at this point! You can experiment.

Keep in mind the idea of a beginning, a middle, and an end to your paper. What might come first? What might come next? What might come last? There are many ways to organize papers, but here are a few most-used ones:

☐ **Time.** The paper is put in order of what happened first in time, what happened next, and what happened last. "First I took the bus downtown, then I went shopping, then I came home."

☐ **Steps.** This is a good way to organize a "how-to" paper. You describe the steps you take in the order you take them. This is the way cookbooks are written.

☐ **Logic.** You can order the material according to its own logic. This book was organized in a logical fashion. There are three big areas of study skills students need to have: study skills they use in class, study skills they use at home, and study skills they use to take tests.

Make an Outline

After you've shuffled your cards a bit, an order for your paper has probably started to appear.

Switch now to paper and pencil and start working out an "outline." We wrote "outline" in quotes, because again, this does not have to be final. An outline is only another tool to get your ideas flowing. If you write it down one way, you don't have to live with it that way forever. You can change it.

FOOD BREAK

Take a food break. Go raid the re-
frigerator for something healthy.
Spend five minutes cutting up and
munching on carrots. Or spread
peanut butter on apple slices. Enjoy!

Write Away!

Actually starting to write can be really scary, too. But remember: you can always change what you write.

Consider your writing a first draft. Leave great big margins all around the paper so you can add things if you want. If you're using lined paper, skip a line and write on every other line. Don't worry if this seems to look like kindergarten. Nobody's going to see it but you. You'll recopy your finished version.

Then, just let your words flow. Actually, writing is not so bad once you've done the kind of organizing we described.

And don't hesitate to change your outline if the paper goes another way when you start writing it. The outline is only a tool.

A tip: if you can type, and someone you know has a word processor, write your paper on the word processor. It's a lot easier than writing it by hand or typing it. Writing on a word processor is like working with clay. You can push, pull, shove, and massage your clay around until you get it just the way you want it. You never have to worry about making a "mistake." You can always fix it.

If you don't know how to type or use a word processor, learn how—quick! The sooner you do, the easier all your papers will be to write, from junior high to high school and beyond.

Writing Leads

Your lead paragraph has to do two things. It has to 1) catch the reader's attention, and 2) introduce the topic. Here's a sample lead.

> After five weeks, two days, and three hours of remaining untouched by vacuum cleaner, dustmop, or dustrag, my room looked like the set for the movie Frankenstein. Little fuzzy cobwebs hung from the ceiling. Gray film dusted the desk, the dresser, and the chair. On the floor there were shirts, books, socks, papers, jeans, soda bottles, magazines, and empty snack wrappers. I decided it was time to clean.

Writing the Body

In the body of your paper, you develop your topic, paragraph by paragraph.

Each paragraph has a topic sentence and several supporting sentences.

Here's the paragraph that follows the lead paragraph on "Cleaning My Room" above.

First I had to clean up the junk on the floor. I decided to start with the clothes. I picked up all the clothes and put them in the laundry hamper. Then I picked up all my books, magazines, and papers. I put them away where they belonged. That left the garbage. I got a big plastic garbage bag and stuffed all the junk into it. Now I was ready to tackle the dirt.

The topic sentences of the remaining paragraphs of this short paper read like this:

- I decided to start with the cobwebs at the top of the room and work down.

- Next I tackled the layer of dust on the desktop and dresser.

- Finally, I hauled out the vacuum cleaner and went after the floor.

Can you tell what each paragraph will be about? Does the paper seem to make sense as a whole? What method of organization was used?

Writing the Conclusion

A concluding paragraph, sentence, or sentences wraps up your paper as neatly as tying a bow on a package. The conclusion can be just that—a logical conclusion you came to as a result of working through your paper. Or it can be the last thing you did, the results of your efforts, or something you learned.

Here's the conclusion to the paper above.

It took me three hours, forty minutes, and sixteen seconds to clean my room after letting it go so long. I spent most of that time just sorting through the junk on my floor. I decided it would be much easier, quicker, and more efficient to keep my room picked up and cleaned up as I go along. A half hour every week is a much better way to go!

PARENT BREAK

Take a parent break. This one will really amaze you. Go talk to one of your parents for five minutes. Find out how his or her day went. They'll be so shocked they might even offer to help you with something on your homework!

A Few More Writing Tips

After you've finished your first draft, go back over your paper. Make it better where you can. Here are a few ways to improve any writing.

☐ **Use the active voice.** "He hit the ball" is the active voice. "The ball was hit by him" is the passive voice. For lively, readable writing, always use the active voice.

☐ **Use strong verbs.** Look at the lead paragraph on page 89. The verb "hung" is strong; "were on" would have been weak. The verb "dusted" is strong; "covered" would have been weak.

☐ **Use concrete nouns.** A concrete noun is one you can see. It's specific, not vague. Again, in that first paragraph, the writer uses "the desk, the dresser, and the chair," which are concrete. "Everything" would have been vague. "Shirts, books, socks, papers," etc. is specific. "Junk" or "stuff" would have been vague.

ACTIVE

STRONG

CONCRETE

☐ **Avoid too many adjectives and adverbs.** A few adjectives and adverbs are fine. Too many, though, and your work becomes cluttered.

☐ **Avoid clichés.** If the writer had said her room "looked like a cyclone had hit it," that would have been a cliché. Instead, she looked for a newer idea, and came up with "a set for the movie *Frankenstein*."

☐ **Make sure your paper is written or typed neatly.** Leave one-inch margins all the way around. If you've had to erase or make a typing correction, be sure they have been done neatly. Make sure your cat hasn't walked on the paper or your baby brother hasn't left gooey fingerprints on it.

☐ **Read your paper one more time.** Make sure you've spelled everything correctly, and that all the punctuation is right. If you're not sure of the spelling, check the dictionary. If you're not sure of the punctuation, check your grammar book.

☐ **Read your paper out loud.** Does it sound smooth?

☐ **Have a friend read your paper.** Four eyes are better than two at catching errors.

Do these last few things and your grade will shine for sure.

What is the main idea?

WRITING BOOK REPORTS

Many teachers will ask you to write reports on books you've read. Often they will give you a form to fill out. If not, be sure to cover these ideas in at least one or two paragraphs per report:

☐ **The theme of the book.** What was the book about? What main idea did you get? Robert Newton Peck's *A Day No Pigs Would Die* is about a son's relationship with his father, and how he must grow up when his father dies.

☐ **The main characters of the book.** Robert, the boy, is the main character in *A Day No Pigs Would Die*. The other main characters are his father, Haven Peck, his mother, Lucy Peck, and his pet pig, Pinky.

☐ **Other characters.** Other characters in *A Day No Pigs Would Die* include the Pecks' neighbor, Mr. Tanner, and Robert's aunt, Carrie.

☐ **What you learned from the book.** This is something you may need to think about a bit. What one person learns from the book will probably be different from what another person learns. For instance, from *A Day No Pigs Would Die*, you might learn how important your relationship is with your parents. Or you might learn how hard but exciting it is to grow up.

☐ **Conclusion.** You might want to conclude your report by listing a few reasons you would or would not recommend that others read the book.

GIVING AN ORAL REPORT

The first part of giving an oral report is similar to writing a paper. You need to research your subject, take notes, and probably make an outline.

After that, it's different.

We speak differently than we write. The chances are that if you wrote out your whole report the way you would a written paper, your speech would not sound natural. It would sound as if you'd memorized it.

So, instead of writing it all out, write short phrases. Put the phrases on note cards, and use the note cards to jog your memory. Then practice giving your speech or oral report out loud.

Stand in front of the mirror, or have one of your study partners be your audience. Then talk through what you want to say. Do it several times, until it comes smoothly.

Do your main practice about two days before your speech. One day before, go over your speech one more time. That way, you'll be ready to speak well in front of the group.

As you get up to give your speech, you'll probably feel nervous. That's natural. Before you start, take a very deep breath. Exhale. Cough if you need to. These things will relax you and open up your throat so that you can speak normally and comfortably.

When you speak, glance at your note cards occasionally. The rest of the time, look at your audience. Remember, they're just your friends. Relax, and you'll do fine.

COMPLETING ASSIGNMENTS OR HANDOUTS

A lot of your homework will simply involve filling in handouts, working problems, writing up experiments, or other writing assignments. Here's how to stay on top of your written assignments.

☐ **Read over the directions before you start.** Be sure you know exactly what the teacher wants you to do on the assignment. It would be awful to get halfway

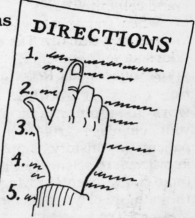

through and realize that you were supposed to skip a line between each problem.

☐ **Skim over the whole handout or assignment before you start.** Which part looks the hardest? Start there if possible, and save the easiest till last.

☐ **If the whole handout or assignment will take you more than a half hour to complete, break it into smaller sections.** Do one section, take a ten-minute break, then do the next section.

☐ **When you finish, quickly check over your work.** Is there anything you could have done better? Did you miss something?

☐ **Be sure your work is neat.** Neatness does count!

☐ **Be sure to apply learning from one class to another class' homework assignment.** Go ahead and use your language arts spelling skills for papers in history. Apply your math knowledge to science assignments. Use a topic you've been studying in science as the subject of your theme for language arts.

FRIENDS IN NEED

Should you ever study with your friends?

The answer can be yes—if both (or all) of you are serious about studying. Most of us learn best when we read something and then talk about what we've read. Getting together with friends to go over a tough reading assignment can be a great way to really get a grasp on it. You can also read each other's papers and offer helpful suggestions or listen to each other practice giving oral reports.

Be sure everyone has read the assignment first. Then get together for a half hour or so to discuss it. Ask each other questions about what you don't understand.

Another idea is to break the reading up into several segments and assign one segment to each study group member. When your study group gets together, everyone gives a detailed report on their segment. This works well for long reading assignments. But don't try it unless all your friends are as good a student as you are.

Of course, you can't write each other's papers or do each other's handouts. But you can get together and brainstorm topics for papers. And you can read each other's finished papers to make sure there are no spelling or punctuation errors.

However you work it, be sure your friends are just as serious about studying as you are. If someone seems to be freeloading on the study group, talk to him about it. If he doesn't beef up his performance, ask him to leave the study group.

Tutoring each other is another way you can study with another student. Maybe you have a friend who needs help in English, but who's good in math. You, on the other hand, need help in math but are good in English. The two of you could agree to tutor each other. Tutoring is a great way to learn. It's been said that you never really know a subject well until you can teach it.

SPECIAL SUBJECTS

Certain subjects call for a few extra study skill tips. Take a look at these ideas for some of your different classes.

Math

Math is very exact and logical. You can't afford to miss or poorly understand a single step. So:

☐ **Rely on rote memory.** Remember learning the multiplication tables with flash cards? Consider making your own flash cards now, for everything from fractions to algebra. They can be small so you can carry them in your pocket. And whenever you have a few spare minutes, you can whip them out and review.

☐ **Ask the teacher.** If there's some step or principle you're just not getting, go to the teacher and have her/him explain it until you do. Don't just let it go. You can't afford to.

☐ **Get a partner.** Study with a friend who's a math whiz. Or find an adult who can give you some math tips. Maybe your parents know someone who's good at math—an accountant or engineer.

Science

Science classes often rely on lab experiments in class. Don't be shy about getting hands-on experience—whether it's formaldehyde frogs or electrical wiring. Then, at home:

☐ **Review.** Write up notes on what you learned in the lab. Don't count on just your memory of the experience, as strong as it may be.

☐ **Visit places of interest.** Consider visiting museums, planetariums, or other scientific displays on your own time. Visiting these displays is a fun and easy way to pick up extra scientific knowledge.

107

Foreign Language

You know you're making progress in a foreign language when you start thinking in it! It might help to make learning a language a game. At home:

☐ **Make comments to your family in your foreign language.** You can even insult them with a smile on your face and they won't know what you've said!

☐ **Talk to yourself half in English, half in your foreign language.** Try to fill in as much of your sentences in the foreign language as you can.

☐ **Visit a part of your city where they speak your foreign language.** See how many signs you can read. Go to a restaurant. Try to read the menu. Try to talk to the waiter or waitress.

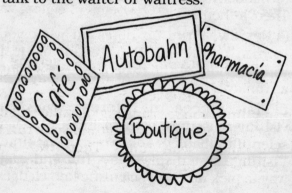

MOVING AHEAD

The biggest difference you'll find in doing homework for the next grade up is that there is more of it. Not only will you have more subjects, but you'll have slightly more to do in each one.

You'll need a slightly longer time to devote to homework. This may be a bit of a jolt to you at first. But soon, as you keep at it, you'll find you ease right into the routine.

You'll probably also find that after the first jolt, the amount of homework you get over your next few years of school will increase fairly gradually.

Not only that, but your abilities grow with the work. It's sort of like getting in shape to run a mile. At first it may seem really hard. But as you keep at it, soon you find you're running a mile easily. Then, gradually, you lengthen your run to one and a half miles. Then two. And before you know it, you're running five miles. You can do it!

Take an art break. Grab your kid sister's crayons and draw a scribble drawing. It doesn't have to be wonderful! It's just for fun and to get some of your energy out.

4
You Can Do Better ON TESTS

It's time for the test. Did you absorb the material from the last week or the last few weeks? How well are you going to do? If you're like most people, your stomach probably gets jittery and your palms start to sweat when you hear the teacher announce a test.

But relax! By keeping your cool and following our pointers, you can do well.

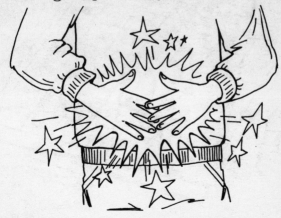

HOW TO STUDY FOR A TEST

One of the most important things about studying for a test is to *begin now*.

Let's say it's Monday and your teacher tells you there will be a test on Friday. That means you have four evenings to study before Friday comes. If you're smart, you'll *study a little bit each day*. Don't leave it all until Thursday night!

Or suppose your teacher has handed out a class schedule at the beginning of the semester. If you're smart, you'll mark the test dates on your calendar. Then you can begin studying about a week and a half before a big test.

What's wrong with waiting until the last minute to study? Your poor brain can't possibly absorb and review all it has to in one quick shot the night before a test. We all learn best in several sessions spread over a length of time. So give your brain a break. Don't expect it to do miracles for you the night before. Treat it well by studying gradually and it will perform well for you on the big test day.

Here's what to do with your test study time.

☐ **To begin.** Be clear. Be very sure exactly what the test will cover. Ask your teacher if you need to. You don't want to waste time reviewing chapters that won't be on the test.

☐ **Four days before.** Review readings. Look over the readings the same way you originally did—scanning the heads, etc.—for their major ideas. Look at your underlined material.

☐ **Three days before.** Review your notes. Take a colored felt-tip marker or highlighter and circle or underline key material in your notes.

Reviewing your readings and reviewing your notes are both very important steps to take in organizing your material so you can begin to memorize it.

☐ **Two days before.** Start memorizing. See the tips below.

☐ **The night before.** Go over your material again to refresh your memory. Did you know that you will forget most of what you are going to forget in the first several hours? To really keep your memory up, you might try this. If the test is first thing in the morning, wake up for a half hour during the night and review the material for the test. You should be able to fall right back asleep and have the benefit of more recent review. If the test is later in the day, find a way to review briefly during the day. You might consider eating your lunch in a quiet corner and studying there. Or maybe you'll have a study hall where you can review.

Test Date is: Friday, May 8

	What I Need to do	Estimated Time
4 Days Before	Review readings from Chapters 5 to 7	1 hour
3 Days Before	Review Notes	45 min.
2 Days Before	Memorize	1½ hrs.
The Day Before	Review memory work	30 min.

STORY BREAK

Take a story break. Slide your favorite book off the shelf. Thumb through it and spend five minutes reading your favorite part. (Promise yourself you'll reread it as a reward for getting a good grade on your next test or homework assignment.)

HOW TO MEMORIZE

No matter what kind of test you will be taking—true/false, multiple choice, or essay—memorizing will help you get through it. You'll be under pressure when you're taking the test, and you simply won't have time to sit there and wonder, "Now let's see—three of the main constellations of spring were—um, well . . . ." The answers need to snap right into your mind.

Here are some memory tips.

☐ **Acrostics.** An easy way to memorize is to put things into lists, and then make one word out of their beginning letters. Suppose you wanted to remember these spring constellations: Gemini, Leo, Ursa Major, and Virgo. In that order, the first letters of each of their names spell GLUV. Remember the word GLUV (and it's strange spelling).

☐ **Association.** Associating the thing you're trying to remember with a mental image, a sound, or a funny word helps you remember it, too. For example, suppose you are trying to memorize the name of the heroine in *Julie of the Wolves* by Jean Craighead George. The heroine's name is *Miyax*. Suppose you sound that out as "me yaks" and picture yourself gabbing on the telephone. "Me yaks." Now you won't forget the heroine's name!

☐ **Numbers.** If you have to remember numbers, especially long ones, break them down into groups of three or four, just like a telephone number. Then memorize one cluster at a time.

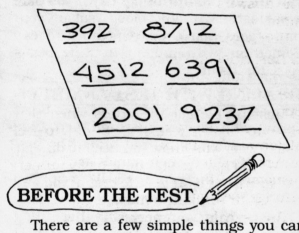

392   8712

4512 6391

2001 9237

BEFORE THE TEST

There are a few simple things you can do to improve your performance on any test.

☐ **Get a good night's sleep.** If you want to, get up in the middle of the night for a half-hour refresher. But don't stay up all night or even half the night. You're likely to fall off your chair in the middle of the test if you do.

☐ **Eat a good breakfast.** Did you know that your body's blood sugar never catches up the rest of the day if you skip breakfast? Without blood sugar your brain goes blank. So remember to eat! Something with protein in it is best—eggs, for instance.

DEALING WITH TEST ANXIETY

Most people get the jitters when they have to take a test. It's natural to feel shaky when you know you need to do well.

But you have to stay on top of your nervousness, not let it get the best of you and block your thinking ability.

To help calm your nerves try this:

☐ **Take several deep breaths.** Exhale slowly and fully.

BROTHER/SISTER BREAK

Take a brother/sister break. Go tickle your baby brother or sister. Have a wrestling match with your grade school brother or sister. You might even consider bugging (mildly!) your older brother or sister.

☐ **Gently tell your body to relax.** Tell your body to relax all the way down to the tips of your fingers and your toes. If your stomach is nervous or if there's any other part of your body that feels tense, gently tell it to relax, too.

☐ **Think positive thoughts.** Tell yourself—and believe it—that you will do just fine on this test.

HOW TO TAKE THE TEST

Applying the Study Key

You knew the good old study key would come in handy again, didn't you? As you sit down to the test, *think big, think medium,* and *think little.*

☐ **Think big.** First of all, read the directions. Look over the entire test. See what you're in for overall.

☐ **Think medium.** Assign periods of time to each of the different sections of the test. Be sure to leave a few minutes for reviewing your work at the end of the test. You might want to actually note down a schedule on a slip of paper and keep it in front of you.

☐ **Think little.** Go to it! Work on the individual questions. Then, before you hand the test in, be sure to look over your work one more time. You just never know what you might catch!

Types of Tests

You'll be taking several different kinds of tests. There will be slightly different things to do in each of these.

True/False

☐ **Watch out for words like *all, never, always.*** They will usually make the most true-sounding statement be false.

☐ **Your first response is usually your best.** If you start stewing over a question, you're more likely not to get it.

Multiple choice

☐ **Be sure to read all the choices carefully and choose the best answer.** Sometimes more than one answer might sound correct.

☐ **Be clear on the directions.** Sometimes on a multiple choice test, the teacher will ask you to choose the *two* best answers. Or one of the answers itself will say, "Both A and C."

Fill in the blank (short answer)

☐ **Watch for grammatical clues.** If the blank is preceded by the word "an," then the answer must begin with a vowel.

☐ **If you can't fill in a blank, move on to the next question.** The answer will probably come to you before you finish the test.

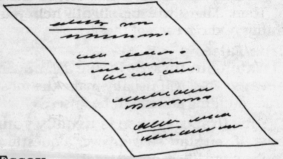

Essay

☐ **Follow your time schedule closely.** It's easy to get carried away writing a terrific essay for the first question and shortchange yourself on time for the next three.

☐ **Use the same format to write an essay as was described in the writing papers section.** Write a strong topic sentence for your paragraph. Then include good supporting details. If your essay is more than several paragraphs long, write an interesting lead, a body of several paragraphs with topic sentences, and a conclusion.

One more hint: When you get your test back, learn from what you did right—and from what you might have missed. Talk to your teacher about your work on the test. Then, *save* the exam. It will help you on the next one!

Take a walk break. Toss on your coat or slip on your sandals and pop out the door. A quick walk around one block—or even two—can really clear your head.

WALK BREAK

MOVING AHEAD

When you move to the next grade up, the biggest switch will probably be that you'll have more essay tests. More and more, teachers will be looking for your ability to think and express yourself in writing.

The paper-writing skills you learned in this book will help you write these tests. You've learned how to organize your thoughts and express them. And, believe it or not, you can still use your memorizing skills to write essays. You can memorize lists of the main things you want to say.

You may also find that your teachers will give midterm exams and final exams. These are big tests that may count for much of your final grade. By applying what you've learned in this book about starting to study early, you'll be able to do very well on big tests like these.

YOUR BEST SHOT

Well, congratulations. You've gotten to the end of this book! The road to getting good grades is a lot like reading this book. You just keep at it—and pretty soon, you get where you're gong. Give it your best shot. You can do it.